CSU Poetry Series LVI

In Joanna's House

46 poems by Bonnie Jacobson

Cleveland State University Poetry Center

ACKNOWLEDGMENTS

My thanks to the editors of these magazines and anthologies in which versions of Joanna poems appear:

THE GETTYSBURG REVIEW: "The Joanna Caper," "Does Joanna Exist?"

THE IOWA REVIEW: "Penelope Joanna"

POCKET POEMS #3 (Bottom Dog Press): "Partytime, Joanna—"

POETRY DIGEST: "The Invitation," "Slender Moon in Sarasota," "The Fugitive"

POTPOURRI: "Circles"

RATTLE: "The Good Ship *Joanna*" (with the title *The Joanna*), "The Invitation," "The
    Face," "Pandora Joanna"

TAR RIVER POETRY: "Charm"

TRIBUTARIES: "Joanna at Her Britannica" (with the title "Fact & Fable")

And thank you to the editors of the bicentennial anthology VOICES OF CLEVELAND
(1996, Cleveland State University Poetry Center) who awarded "Joanna Raises Her Shade"
their $500 first prize.

Indispensable to the writing and assembling of this book have been: my husband Aaron
Jacobson, my daughter Mia Stromberg, and my friends Robert Wallace, Lolette Kuby and
all members of the Butcher Shop.

Manufactured in the United States of America

Published by Cleveland State University Poetry Center
1983 East 24th Street
Cleveland, OH 44115-2440

ISBN 1-880834-42-1

Library of Congress Catalog
Card Number: 98-72251

CONTENTS

IN JOANNA'S HOUSE

PROLOGUE: ENDING JOANNA

Now we are dropping her collection of Spode.
We are stripping her cherrywood closets,
shredding her cruisewear, her politics.
Now we are canceling her fingerprints,
her memberships in class and color.
We are confiscating her gender, her charities,
her symphonies, beginning with Mahler,
even Beethoven. There go her favorite flora,
lilacs from Whitman, scallions from God.
Shalom, God, nothing personal—we are
uprooting her new guru too, burning
the saint that in time she hoped to become,
burning time and the phoenixes of time.
Time will not rise as space nor as eternity either.
(Time has no direction of its own.)
Now we are disconnecting her people.
The brightest, the warmest, fizzle and fade.
Though she tries, she cannot find their arms, nor care,
for now we are pumping love from her heart,
plunging into her gut, scooping out rage,
mopping up shame, drawing the taffeta drapes.
We have squashed the fear that buzzed on her sill.
Her mirror is empty. She knows nothing.
She expects nothing. She is complete, ready.
Now we are taking ourselves away.
It never worked, *anyone's* identity.

I

HOW SHE GREW

Once she *began,* Joanna believes.
Cold and wet, unable to tell herself from
the air, or the shore, or the two lovers
who held her and sang to her, who called her
their answered prayer, their wee naked beauty
sprung from the sea: *relax,* they sang.
And so for an opulent while with no time in it
she played with her mind as if mind were
the whole playful universe, her oyster
and her pearl. She was one bundle of love
expecting nothing less; a year later
her hands were literally in the cake, she has
the pictures to prove it. But only the greatest
of saints and sinners can live like this,
Joanna believes. In time, she learned who she was—
a child who did not touch the bisque figurines,
a girl who agreed with her teacher.
Under her cap and gown, her wedding veil,
holding her little ones, Joanna smiles at
the photographer's finger, how easy this is,
smiling atop the Steinway, smiling in her
husband's wallet. Here, she is caught in
a gilt-edged mirror, smiling at her smile.
Lady, she seems to be saying, I know you,
but I know you only to the extent
that it serves my purpose.

THE INVITATION

A strange woman came to Joanna's house.
She wore no makeup and a panama hat.
She asked Joanna what Joanna
wanted to do with the rest of her life.
"Claret or tea?" Joanna said and left
to fetch the rolled sandwiches, each with
an olive slice in its middle, like an owl eye
or a fish eye, which is exactly how
the woman's eyes looked to Joanna, too wide,
too expectant. If there was one thing
Joanna had learned in her relatively
happy half century it was: most questions
left to themselves will answer themselves, for
aren't you born, doesn't one thing lead to
another, and then like a lightbulb don't you
go out—which was to have been Joanna's
reply, but when Joanna reentered with
her filigreed tray and bright smile, there was
only the slightest indentation upon
her Biedermeier sofa's goosedown cushion,
although on the marble table nearby
the crumpled remains of the scented vellum
upon which Joanna had written *Do
join me at three* were imperceptibly
opening—like the petals of an ink-veined
lotus, Joanna was pleased to observe.

DOES JOANNA EXIST?

Of course she exists, everyone says so.
There is a certificate with a seal.
You've seen her jog by, she is blond and slim.
Who would sit down in a chair where she sits?
Look her up, ring the doorbell and ask—
her husband and her children will tell you
Joanna is upstairs in her sitting room,
happily stitching twelve birds into twelve
dining room chairseats, thinking of all those
who will sit upon her birds, and would gladly
pop down if you think otherwise.
But why should you think otherwise?
What sort of world would this be if you
(or anyone, surely Joanna herself)
were to find after a lifetime lived
otherwise that Joanna is not the creature
all had assumed, but is in reality
some weird emanation from eternity
sealed up in a mind that *thinks* it's Joanna,
a body that lives in Joanna's house?
To whose advantage if everything known
is wrong? Joanna might have to resign
from her club, her charity boards, her friends
forced to dine elsewhere, her family regroup—
Of course she exists, everyone sighs.
And you exist too, Joanna replies.

HAPPY JOANNA

There is no good reason for Joanna
not to be happy. She has always been
happy. It is her duty, her talent
and her prize. When Joanna is happy
it makes her parents happy (the milky
burble; the wedding album on their table).
It makes her husband and her children
happy, and all those fortunate to be
in Joanna's vicinity, happy,
from the supermarket cashier to the
maid who boogaloos in her kitchen.
And you know how the pebble impresses
the pond—the cashier will pass along
Joanna's smile, the maid will smile upon
her own fine children. There is just enough
truth to this to make Joanna wonder
if in her daily intercourse she might
spread an epidemic of happiness,
a chain letter all the way to the White House
and beyond, the whole planet exploding
with happiness, the founding fathers
and God in his heaven, supremely happy.
In which case, it is imperative
that Joanna stay happy, for every
death depends upon her, every failed
hope, every sad and desperate thing, *hers*.

WEE JOANNA AND THE BROTHERS GRIMM

When the wind has had its whirl, danced all night
in the arms of the elms and littered the walk
with twigs from their latest mazurka,
then mama snaps the red galoshes
and wee Joanna sweeps. If the wind came
dressed in rain, wee Joanna heaps wet
kindling by the pantry door where it suns
like a party of snakes and dries like
mama's hair when she dips it in vinegar
and spreads it like a fan. In mama's kitchen
the stove stands on little dog legs, water
runs chuckling from the tap, and the hen leaps
in the pot. On drowsy afternoons when
wee Joanna climbs into mama's lap,
the good girls always marry the prince.
And someday a prince for Joanna, mama says.
Once mama read The-bad-girl-who-ran-off-
to-see-a-witch. *Little girl, little girl,
why so pale,* mama read. *O witch, I peeped in
at your window and saw a fiery head.
Then you have seen me in my proper dress,*
frowned the witch and turned the little girl into a log
and threw the log into her fire crying,
Now at last I am warm! Oh that silly girl,
mama sighed (and wee Joanna sighed too)—
she did not mind her mother.

BEING GOOD

No grownup taught her Original Good,
or even that virtue might be delicious,
a real roll in the hay, the mooning of
every magistrate, every warden.
No wonder she confuses *good* with *nice*
and *nice* with *obedient.* No wonder
she thinks she is good when she does not do
what she wants to do, especially good
when she does what others need her to do,
though gratification is tricky. For example,
duty feels much less saintly than impulse.
Sainthood is easy, an activist friend
once told Joanna, you know what is right
and then you do it. Joanna was shocked.
Her definition of a saint was someone
perpetually better than herself.
She did not know everybody was in the running.
For a while Joanna struggled to determine
what was right, in order to act upon
her certitude. And then she gave it up.
One morning, late for a charity brunch,
she wrestled open the closing doors
of a downtown elevator and a man inside
mumbled, "Wow, I could never do that."
"You must not denigrate yourself,"
Joanna told him. But that just slipped out.

FREUD TELLS JOANNA

Today Freud is teaching her Shakespeare,
explaining Lear and Cordelia. (Always,
Freud has tried his best to teach her everything—
early on he told her, *Your ego serves*
three tyrants, the external world,
the superego and the id.) For her part,
Joanna is rapt, grateful for Freud's indulgence,
though she fidgets when he speaks in threes
as in the trinity, or fairy tales.
Eternal wisdom bids Lear renounce love,
choose death and make friends with
the necessity of dying, Freud is saying.
Joanna asks, Did Cordelia choose death too?
How could she, Cordelia is death, Freud explodes,
you failed to reverse *the scene—Lear is*
the fallen hero Cordelia carries to Valhalla.
Joanna is mortified. Once again
she has got it wrong. *Completely,* Freud sighs.
Man has three relationships with women:
the mother who bears him, the companion of
his bed and board, and—Freud aims
his finger at Joanna—*the destroyer!*
Joanna studies her hands folded in her lap.
She feels she has never harmed a living soul.
Yet she must have done something—
this brilliant man is unhappy with her.

THE FACE

Joanna cannot satisfy herself.
She looks this way and that, oppressed by *Vogue.*
In Joanna's culture the women paint
a face on their faces, an inhuman one
perfect as an egg, this is the face they ape.
It comes to them monthly, steeled as a saint's,
pornographic as a child's, sprung grownup
from its little pots of venus flytrap,
its pearlhandled brush and smudges of kohl,
that its eyes like mothwings may open to
astonish. Wherever the women go,
the doctor's, the grocer's, the reading room
of their public library, it stares like
J. Edgar Hoover into their happiness.
While they shower, it lies on their nightstands
and ogles their husbands, this is their fear.
While they suckle their infants, it jets to
a market in Madagascar where urchins
reach for its glittering, this is what they are
up against. The immaculate concept.
The immortal fuschia pout. The face that
when their own faces crack and begin to leak through
will sit on the supple spine of a trout
and mock them, the face still flirting with
intimacy, still fleeing from page to page
on its barely possible giraffe legs.

SLENDER MOON IN SARASOTA

Joanna knows her, this professional.
This model striding in palest blue sandals
across a blueblack marbled sea.
Tonight she shows a sky of grey Egyptian linen
(a dinner sky, more charcoal than pewter
and worn with stars). Her fabled float, her crisp
pause beyond the tennis court, her demi-turn
and turn again, her nod to the blazing
turquoise pool and the jade lattice of fronds
(the best jade, the deepest green) are above
reproach, to which she adds her impromptu
over-the-shoulder smile, a Garbo tease,
witty, as if she were about to speak.
It is an old rebuke, she will not speak—
she is too elegant for words, this moon.
She is a paradigm of moon, though not
the only one. Moons less elegant have thrilled:
fat moons, moons naked, bald as an egg.
So why does Joanna dress hers like this,
in the elegance of a sea-length gown?
If the truth of beauty were known, is elegance
like armor, like some lovely layered shell,
and inside that mother-of-pearl room
the quivering worm *shame?* Or is it
an act of reverence to braid the glossy night,
to nest magnolias at the nape?

PARTYTIME, JOANNA—

Time to curry the eggs and mull the wine.
Set up the cellist and stir the spouse.
Fluff the children and fling open the door
to all those who have flung open theirs, beaming
welcome to our privacy, slip from your wrap
yes I can see yours is an enviable blouse
so lovely this occasional intimacy
have you met let us pour we're just back.
Time to gather at the window and *look at that*
another sun is dying *always so sad*
when its red eye sinks *titanic but what*
can you do night is a bitch and promiscuous
—or so the olive gossips on the stem,
so the hour murmurs, so the eyes move in the room—
Oh where is it *the time of our lives?*
Quick, Joanna, light another candle,
light a crystal chandelier, a crackling fire,
a pêche flambée. Insist they *cannot go*
and embrace them as they go. Wave, wave
to the lingerers handed into their cars,
wave to their slim parade through the gate.
Then walk the dog slowly. Pause.
The Dipper is stars pouring stars.
They are more beautiful than they know.
And the last crystal fragments of snow.
And the dog, ready now to curl and sleep.

THE ULTIMATE DINING ROOM

Joanna's dining room is large enough.
It has enough silver, enough linen,
enough needlepoint chairs (twelve of them).
And hanging just above Joanna's head,
when Joanna ladles bouillabaisse, is her
great-grandfather-the-fish-merchant's head,
allowed to gaze morosely from its frame
at the plates from which he once ate.
Sometimes, though, ambition nibbles at Joanna.
Why not heavier silver, older chairs,
a greater great-grandfather? Is modesty
her fatal flaw? Or is it dread of mazes
meant to hide the greatest of dining rooms
from all but the cleverest of hostesses
(*which* caterer, *which* florist, *which* guest list)?
Will Joanna's dining room never grow
larger, never move from lawn to park to empire
for that one delicious moment when
a hostess enters the ultimate room,
the dining room at the top, where hostesses
never walk, but, ugly ducklings no more, they *glide*—
And once there, do they dine alone in
the only dining room in the world in which
no one wants anything anymore? Is it like
the Sargasso Sea where a carnivorous weed
eats the fish that came to eat it?

THE POOLSIDE BALLET

JOANNA'S TOWEL unfurls in a tour jeté
as NOON enters and exits
followed instantly by a brisance of
MOMENTS, those various gnomes and undines,
pert salamanders and nixes, wilis,
peris and sprites, all nimbler than the eye,
their everpresent fouettés and bourrées
a precision of limbs and wings rushing, teasing,
turning, chasing, flickering, fading
and reappearing, their blunt shoes ticking.
Contrapuntally, WALL, PALM and CHAIR
in a bold example of tableau vivant
do not move from their marks.
Rather, WALL engages WALL,
PALM, PALM and CHAIR, CHAIR
in a furious divertissement of containment.
Then, slowly, majestically, the dark and brooding
CORPS DE L'OMBRE begin their tortured advance—
WALLSHADOW extending to PALM—
PALMSHADOW extending to CHAIR—
CHAIRSHADOW extending almost, but never, to
POOL, a vision so azure, so fluid,
a figure so deep and yet transparent,
JOANNA cannot contain herself.
An indulgent CHAIR bids her adieu as
enchanted, JOANNA leaps and glides forth, a swan at last.

JOHN CALVIN TELLS JOANNA

Alas, Joanna, you can never be Presbyterian.
Though you have the sin for it,
the blond hair and the voice within for it,
though our sermon of Christian fellowship
makes your heart sing, you cannot kneel with
us after, or ride to our Sunday picnic.
Not in this life, Joanna. In this life
God wants you to ride with the Jews, a cross
any one of us might have been handed.
Protest not, Joanna. God believes
you protest too much. Only yesterday
while strolling His pastures, God said to me,
John, what is this nervous complaint
wherein Joanna pictures a black boot
that splinters her door and drags her forth,
her teakettle screaming, her brick steps,
her roses, bleeding under her knees,
her good neighbors mute, et cetera.
God says he is sick of hearing that story,
and besides, there are certain rules of logic:
Joanna cannot be two religions at once,
nor all religions either, that's really crazy.
Remind her: Salvation is a private club,
its members picked at birth; lovely,
with a dungeon underneath, so deep
the blessed cannot hear the damned cry out.

IF JOANNA KNEW GOD'S PLAN

If Joanna knew God's plan was no more
than this—a fistful of dust flung at nothing
and for no other reason than: something
perfect includes disarray—and if one mote
got carried away, if in its split-second suspension
that mote entered Time, and Dimension,
fell into Cooling and Curdling, and if
in that curdle ambitious humps and hairs
ate of each other and grew shrewder,
and if the shrewdest of these told God
God loved what He had done, how His torso
had swiveled, His arm had swung in a
purposeful arc, much as a potter casts his clay,
said the shrewdest, God so pleased with
His amphoras, His tankards, His teacups
and funerary urns—the red-figured,
the black-figured, the crackled and cloisonnéd—
that when His vessels fell, as vessels will,
when they were dust upon a dusty hill,
God would gather their dust and fling them again,
careful to save the best for His shelves,
because, said the shrewdest, *our salvation
is Your plan*—and if Joanna knew God would
merely go in to dinner, His plan no more than
this one idle fistful of dust—she would still
sit among the flowers and rejoice.

PICNIC AT THE SHORE

Then pleasure said, Let us speak candidly.
Let us speak lyrically of in-the-fist money.
Of money in its cool and figgy beauty.
Oil of money, Joanna, drizzled onto
your shoulder, spread along your thigh.
And guilt said, Oh quiet, money's naughty.
Not a fit topic for Presbyterians
or lovers of poetry, guilt said.
You can't take it with you, charity said.
And pleasure said, What *will* you take away?
Will you unscrew the sun, fold up the sea?
Will you be traveling at all, by the way?
Faith does not know, nor hope, obviously.
They do not know the whereabouts of their
own grandmothers, that's their specialty.
Try the new paté, pleasure said.
And modesty said, But money's greedy.
The Delaware Indians lost Manhattan
because they wore more beads than necessary.
Money should be tasteful, modesty said
plucking a grape. And then money spoke up.
Money said gosh it was only money.
Live by the sea with your love, money said.
And the sea said it was only the sea, live with love.
And love said it was only love, live.
And life said it was only life.

II

SNAKE OIL

He knows the right buttons, the salesman
who swears Joanna can go home again,
step in the same river twice. *Brain Tapes,*
he beams, patting his sample case, and if he
might have the loan of her V*CR* plus
a *wee* bit of her time, he guarantees
Joanna will understand *every*thing,
secrets the *big boys* don't want her to know.
Thus, in spite of herself she finds herself
seated next to him on the divan, watching
what turns out to be her whole fuddled life,
each kiss rekissed, each sob resobbed.
So sad, he murmurs, offering tissues,
though *not one* of her faults is her fault,
as tapes of her *parents' lives* would certainly
prove, and *yes* those tapes *are* available,
uncensored and beautifully lit, *plus*
for the scholar there's a family *history* of
failure and mayhem, rare footage all the way back
to Eve, starstruck and grooming herself.
He recommends Joanna buy the set,
and because she is such a nice *person,*
he will throw in his handy remote
so Joanna can rewind, replay, freeze
and minutely examine each trespass and sin
without moving *one* pretty muscle.

JOANNA FALLING

If it is true we are all of us fallen,
none the angel we might have been,
when did she fall, Joanna keeps fussing,
was it *back then* before she existed?
Is she Eve? Or is she the whole sorry story,
a man-woman-God-snake sort of flurry
falling up, down, in place and sideways?
Perhaps she's a page out of Sartre, able to fall
all by herself. Or maybe God pushed her,
took too many she loved, so now she
bribes God with belief, hoping to reunite
in Heaven, a sure sign she has fallen,
this personalizing. Last week while crossing
the mall parking lot Joanna saw a stranger
about to unlock his car *sneeze* and from
a distance *Joanna's* nose felt what the other
nose felt, its tickle and its release, but
as the stranger disappeared into his car
and Joanna continued her walk toward Saks,
she fell back into the habit of being
only Joanna, shopping for something.
And why was it safer—to disengage—
even her question hard to hold onto as
down she goes, having plunged from grace
the day she washed her dumb cousin's face in
the snow, and that was just the beginning.

TO JOANNA, SHOPPING FOR TOWELS

Lady, for shame! This commerce is a crime
when all the May-mad birds are cooing!
Come, Joanna, come at once from Hills and
Bloomingdales, for love runs hot and deathly cold
whilst you admire towels. Ah, but the
blue of them, the peach plum grape
and ecru of them—what canny elves have
picked the orchards bare and stacked their fruit
on lucite everywhere—what shelves are these—
what folded meadows fall to such a sea
where all meander tabled aisles, exchanging
smiles, exchanging sighs, for never since
the world began was beauty so at hand, so
tangible, so necessary—yes, yes, I knew
you'd understand—for, what use are fingertips
if not to read as sculptors read their stone,
as lovers read their own sweet Braille, now his,
now hers, in whorls of thread as soft as
thirsty curls against her breasts, how thick
those curls, velour those breasts—
Oh, in this temple, this museum—even
Sundays, sing *Te Deum*—may we tarry,
may we dream—of rooms where nature
is no guest, but daily you and I, undressed,
shall sport in showers of lemon, lime—
if there are towels enough, and time.

THE AUDIENCE

Here they come, a gaggle of strangers,
a sea anemone settling in,
their faces like petals on a bough,
like facets of an enormous insect eye,
Joanna fifth row on the aisle, wondering
what in the world is she doing here, out
of her depth, for this is no prosaic sea,
this is a sea awaiting its moon-person,
flown in and seated somewhere among them,
soon to rise. *Famous for his paradoxical
simultaneity,* her friend is explaining.
Joanna is glad her friend is here to explain,
though why poetry is beyond her
is beyond her. Sometimes Joanna thinks
poetry is easier than she thinks, because
doesn't an audience know what it needs,
and doesn't it know when it gets it,
herself included? Like a blossoming tree
or bees out for clover, Joanna wants to say.
"Poetry is what we *could* say if we *would,*"
Joanna's friend once said a famous poet
once said, but when Joanna asked her friend
what did the poet mean, was he praising us
or blaming us, was poetry some test
we, but not he, had failed—her friend wouldn't
or couldn't (or shouldn't, who can say?) say.

THE GOOD SHIP *JOANNA*

Upon the body she imposed the soul.
Over the what-is, the what-should-be.
And Joanna's problem lay not in the body,
nor in the soul, but in the distance between.
For Joanna let her soul fly up to Heaven,
Joanna told her body she hoped to sail there
someday (no port so bejeweled
as one seen from afar). Thus, Joanna
became *The Joanna,* tossed on a sea
of ambitious winds: Oh may she end *up*
where her soul is, Heaven in a single gust
(or many crossings if need be, her karma
hauled from life to life until unloaded).
And may her dark nights pulse with blips.
(Are they beacons, or only other ships?)
At the very least, may she float forever
as weeds, water, salt, perhaps a reef of coral,
a deep breath once taken and released.
(How nice that sounds, but is it moral?)
Heavenly tomorrow, when *will* you save today—
Inspired by such talk *The Joanna* sails on,
past Joanna's shallower afternoons,
the dog chasing small crabs out of the foam,
Joanna's hand snagging twixt finger and thumb
some tall ship that crawls the horizon—

JOANNA MERRY IN THE HOUSE OF SORROW

Joanna is Hercules, tough as nails.
Nothing in air, sea or burial ground
can bring her down, not the loud weeping
of her daughter's body, nor the glazed face.
Armies of rabbis came to console her;
she braided their beards and sent them home.
For a time, Joanna dwelt among apes,
for apes in their wisdom do not wrestle from
the breast of a determined mother
the rotting carcass of her child.
Who dares to challenge brute grief and remorse?
Only Joanna was a match for Joanna.
Only Joanna could tunnel from Hades,
leap out and party on the grave of grief,
hire a band and foxtrot her daughter
with a quickstep so funky, laughter
split its sides and death ordered Joanna
to stop, she was making a mockery.
But the couple would not stop: roused,
Joanna's daughter wants Bizet and show tunes,
Sting and African drums; she relocates
home and rocks the house again.
Death, give it up—there's no controlling this child,
on and on she bounces, it's *life* she's after,
Joanna's rattley daughter—
Kumbaya, eight years and still dancing—

WHAT JOANNA WOULD LIKE TO THINK

Years after her death Joanna stands at the edge
of the sea where all things are possible,
if only she had known. She stands with her
husband and children, all of them come
for Joanna's last daughter, an old woman
with children of her own. The sun still favors
their winter retreat, its plush white sand
still cool underfoot, the crystal wake of glaciers.
But the gates of Joanna's island are open.
The summer families are welcome.
Their pomade and guitars worry no one.
They haul Joanna's antique wicker onto the beach.
They plant their umbrellas bright as begonias.
The summer babies shriek and run about
naked as gulls. Clothed to her toes,
Joanna's last daughter lifts her gauze skirt,
extends her wrinkled leg, about to dance in sand.
Nearby, heroes flex, beauties bob in the sea.
All day they dream of touching each other
in Joanna's gazebo where right now
the papas are cooking mullet straight from the net
and the mamas are dishing out chilis and rice.
No one can see Joanna and her family.
What they see—if they see anything—
is an old woman hobbling. They do not know
she is doing the merengué with souls.

JOGGING TO THE INNER CITY

It's a six-hour jog from Joanna's gatehouse
should she wish to suit up and run down there.
She could take her dog, make new friends.
But *already* she loves too many people
not well enough, Joanna pleads, and every day
she meets *more,* at lectures, over cocktails,
like dust, like birds, they're everywhere,
each as exotic as anything under the sea
and all ready to lunch if she's free.
Still, she can picture the run: level at first
and, except for chitchat of cricket, coo of bird,
quiet—the shy people of the Hunt Club
and the gentleman farmer, rarely seen.
At some point the road would drop, houses
moving closer, men on porchsteps, kids
in the street, her last mile like a market crash,
like the splat of an egg, down that hill of tires and bottles—
She'd have to brace herself, skid to a dignified
stop. And once landed, what would she *do,*
hire a guide? Shop? *No, no,* Joanna is saying,
she wants to meet the *locals,* hang with the hood.
But who will make the arrangements, who will
set up the rules? *A committee?* Joanna suggests,
running in place, smiling a lot. But who
will arrange for the committee to meet,
who will set up the rules?

CROWS ON THE BORDER

Raucouser, bigger, bolder each year,
this year they are dead sure
life is as they have always taught,
squarely on their side, and never more
awesomely than right now, for look—on the roof
she once ruled isn't that Joanna's cat queen
cowering, and look, look—on the sycamore branch
that was the queen's private causeway,
haven't the riffraff deployed a mere
two of themselves to depose her, and don't those
two caudillos know that claw for claw
the cause with less to lose wins,
that from this morning on, any waltz
down a royal tree, any saunter
through a civilized door to a civilized bowl
is cat queen history because (poor puss)
she forgot how it feels to be part of a pack,
to terrorize terror till its bloody jaws
are sausage—it feels *immortal,* that's how it feels—
for even when Joanna thinks to raise
the nearest upstairs window don't those two
stare and refuse to budge—and even when
Joanna slams the window shut and
the queen stands tall against the glass
hissing she's free, she's free, don't they
jeer *caught—caught—caught—*

MOTHS

                        So eagerly
a fat, soft moth will enter Joanna's house.
A small distraction, but there it is.
Sometimes Joanna lets it flail,
sometimes she cups its flutter, the buzz
erotic on her skin, the syzygy
jazzy to her ear, impassioned, the whole
tragedy of Giselle in the hollow of her hand.
On those nights, more often than not
(Joanna likes to think) she has
slipped her desperate guest back into
its own spacious house, and on exceptional
nights (twice, at least) Joanna and moth
have escaped altogether—there they go—
gauze and nightgown over the lawn
and into the pure light of the particular body,
two forms ecstatic in wet grassblades
and a sweet southern wind. But sometimes,
in a tic of a mood, a flicker of
inattention, Joanna has crushed its kind.
Given the godliest of intentions
(Joanna would very much like to believe this)
she is not meant to be perfect, nor is she
unique in her imperfection, witness
the soft moths who err so often
and always so eagerly.

JOANNA AT HER BRITANNICA

In Amazonia specialist moths
feed their families from the feces
of the three-toed sloth. Polite as dinner guests,
patient as communicants awaiting the wafer,
the moths hang out in woolly hairs,
profound believers in the sloth's
once-a-week descent from its tree and then
the dump. Life is sweet for the moths.
Over the eons, they have kept their
numbers low, asking of the sloth only
what the sloth can give, shunning
all things exceptional, vague and puzzling,
following instead the narrower path
of contentment. And the grateful sloth,
in whose multi-chambered stomach
its various dinners steep, has remained
their perfect host—a peaceable seeker of leaves,
a meditator nine-tenths of its day,
a mendicant who builds no nest, knowing
anywhere it is is home. *Home, home,* chorus
the moths—both blind monk and acolytes deep
in a place Joanna thinks of as *The Now,*
undisturbed by Joanna's latest fact
that in all of history there is not one fable
praising the discreet way of the sloth
or the long, full lives of moths.

ON FREEWAYS

Freeways lie to you, Joanna found out.
There is no vault where the hours you save
are socked away. Cloverleafs aren't leaves,
they're the coffins of leaves. Not green and lucky,
anything that manipulates. Once she drove
the L.A. Freeway and ended in the twilight zone.
She never was much of a speed reader.
Even in her youth she liked to savor
the names, roll them like grapes: Ana heimm
San Looee O biss po   Marina del RA ee.
And so her California lover never got collected.
He waited all day, but that's all right.
He got where he was going, married a girl
like herself. Two roads diverged and one
seemed better, Joanna sighs, but on freeways
where is the margin for error, the friendly
driveway to borrow like a cup of sugar
where you turn in, and back out, starting
over and righting yourself? Best, she's learned,
to *walk* where you want to go. Know in your bones
where you have been, and where you are going,
and *this* Jersey pine, bending *just so,*
this is where you are now. Each day should be
just long enough. It should feel as if you
are turning the earth with your feet,
turning it with a slow, determined grace.

THE FUGITIVE

33

Hot on the winged heels of the perfect self
Joanna shouts, *You there!* and *Wait for me!*
She tries *Thou,* and then she kicks a tree
because why is Joanna always the person
missing the missing person? Sometimes she's
the pathetic next of kin who leans from
the varnished oak visitor's chair to guide
the police artist's hand (*no, no,* my person's
eyes were deeper, truer, add more
Ghandi, more Mother Teresa, *yes,* lips
like mine but hers outsang the lark, each note
a moon, no moon more fair, last seen
wearing raiment). And sometimes she's
the ballsy supercop who can outlast
the FBI, the CIA, Rambo
and all the local sheriffs though they
batter every door and drag the river twice.
Once in Louisiana Joanna's hounds
had her person surrounded but Joanna
did something clumsy, something so stupid
Joanna's missing person was heard to
snicker from the other side of the swamp,
possibly she had found an old canoe,
was headed down the bayou. *Aw hell, lady,*
Joanna's trackers kept muttering,
why don't you just let her go.

THE GAP BETWEEN FEELING AND ACT

Be good, be good, boomed the big one,
or I will ride a bicycle on your head.

But I am, I am good, whimpered Joanna.

Then be better, bellowed the big one,
or an elephant will swallow your fingers.

Better? Better than what? gulped Joanna.

Better than you are, blistered the big one,
or eight hundred saints will die in your place.

And if I am better? brightened Joanna.

Then be better than better, blared the big one,
or for eternity the 1812
Overture will repeat in your ear.

I am trying, pleaded Joanna,
feeling the great cold foot on her neck,
but the truth is I don't want to be better—
I just want you to go away.

Ah well, that's a whole different story,
said the big one, and went away.

JOANNA FLYING

Anyone can do this, step out onto
the wing of the plane and frolic there
in the snowscape beyond it. Like the saints
and the astronauts already out there,
anyone, from an ancient Nepalese prince
to you, Joanna, dozing over Iowa,
can step from the danger of safety.
Moreover, without leaving the pillow
of your husband's shoulder, you can know
if your flight attendant was right to remove
the young mother with an armful of baby
from the seat nearest the emergency exit
and put in her place the man clutching
his briefcase. You, husband, anyone, can know
if that briefcased man now lost in thought
is your more reliable door opener
because you can enter his mind,
see what he sees, love what he loves—
and if when you enter you find to your horror
despair is a hole he's fallen through
and what stares out the window is only
a shave and some tailoring, you can reach through
and save him, he can be your last sad man,
safe at last in your arms and you safe in his.
One by one, anyone can do this.
And then anyone can do the next thing.

THE JOANNA CAPER

The detective's mysterious client
is innocent, she purrs, pursued by time
who knew her when. He lights her cigarette,
their eyes write a book, maybe *War and Peace*
or *Paradise Lost.* Who is this dame,
the detective is thinking, does she think
she can buy his mind, slowdance with his soul?
Is she Christ in a red silk kimono
or has she iced the detective's partner,
poor sap, found face down in yesterday's blood?
Joanna recrosses her black silk legs.
The detective sighs. He's been through all this
before, these murder mystery trappings
put to metaphysical uses, and where
has it got him—angel or not, the dame
always dies, that's her appeal, she leaves him
exactly where he expects to be left—
beat-up and alone in a bar, nursing his past
like a hangover. What was it last night,
mother's milk or a mickey? The detective
forgets, but his past will remember,
his past will fling him like dollars on the bar,
his past will reel him on, to the next past.
She has a plan, Joanna is saying: They
move to Ohio, plant corn and tomatoes;
she disguises herself with five children.

THINKING SMALL

Joanna is spreading her toast with butter.
It puddles into innumerable craters
which (Joanna is saying to her husband)
tiny explorers might name Big Yellow Lake,
Slippery Gorge, Sweet Cholesterol Pond,
the future stacked in every breadbox,
assuming, of course, there's a shrinking machine,
already in the works, Joanna suspects,
somewhere in Utah and shaped like a gun.
"Umhum," says the Wall Street Journal.
Why, any buttered toast could be a spa
where a million dry-skinned women like herself
might soak themselves. Backpackers could hike
fresh miles of Yellowtoast National Park.
Whole populations, fruit flies and all, could
if they wished be officially shrunk, the starving
fed at last by the crumbs they are thrown.
"Mm," says the coffee cup's bottom.
Think of it, instead of shooting too soon into space,
we could move inward, burrow
in loaves of infinite niches, our children
proliferating from toastsized to
increasingly subquarkian, our lives
nothing like yesterday's market quotations
(Joanna says to the kiss on her cheek)
when *vast* is a buttery speck.

IT WAS A DELICATE SITUATION

In the car of the gynecologist
on the way to his box at the opera
the two gentlemen grew agitated
as happens with a subject like rape.
Nevertheless (Joanna, undressing, would
remind her husband) it was the men
who raised the issue and could not let it drop:
the doctor newly hired by the accused;
Joanna's husband asked to counsel
their host on how to appear the expert witness.
(The two ladies strangers but for this evening.)
Not rape, said the doctor fishing for tickets,
not when they're man and wife and two days before
she consented. The punishment exceeds
the crime, said his counsellor bringing
the ladies their intermission chardonnay,
the ladies discussing the mediocre
performance of that night's Don Giovanni,
the doctor remarking, The bruise on her face
and the bruise on her shoulder might have been
amorous. Or she might have deserved it,
the doctor's wife giggled. Indeed,
Joanna began, it's a terrible thing
when the strong are threatened. What's that,
said the doctor cupping his ear, but a
fretwork of bells was chiming the next act.

DECORATING THE OFFICE

From the silence of antiquity
the artist Wu escaped by painting
on her silk and many-paneled screen
quaint studies of the emperor. Not for
a boardroom, Joanna's husband complains.
Obviously a domestic piece, the dealer
agrees, something your wife might like.
The artist Wu waits for Joanna's reply.
Her strokes warn of wind, Joanna says.
Notice. The emperor's pines, his twittering chimes,
dance for the emperor when wind wishes.
And here. The gull, the dragonfly, the prince
with ribboned kite, play on little legs
wind's game. On summer nights the empress
sighs for wind's embrace, the concubines
turn in their sleep. Worse. When the emperor
flushes the succulent deer, wind takes
his arrow, wind sits in his bowl. What can
he do. When the emperor walls his city
he forbids windows for the wind, but here,
there, wind looks in. When the emperor orders
his admirals to cast wind into the sea, wind
hurls them home. What to do, what to do.
So the emperor summoned the artist Wu.
In a single day Wu captured the sea and the sky
but the image of wind is wind, Wu says.

PENELOPE JOANNA

Once a year Joanna's husband leaves her.
Packs his gear and sails north, in need of setting out
and returning. His friends go too.
Sometimes they see a bear, or dream they do.
Once, on a wilderness island, they knelt
for an hour and watched a snake eat a frog,
its bleat last in. That night they asked themselves
important questions, but drank too much
to remember the answers. He guesses
they spoke of the war, and women, stories
Joanna does not want to hear, he tells her,
and rolls over and turns off the light.
Once Joanna's husband was seized from
his ship and rushed to an insolent port.
There, he was stripped and shaved hairless
as an Arab bride, he was painted yellow
and cracked like an almond, and entered.
He woke a zero, a poor Pinocchio
dangled from wires, a fetus, reborn at last
but wheeled home, the child of his wife.
Yes you may, no you may not, she chirped.
One night while she slept, he slipped from
her slipcovered rooms, he leapt her hedges
and ran off to sea, thrusting north, ice on his beard—
Oh where has he gone, his poor wife cried,
my little hibiscus, my delicate boy—

CHARM

Often, men like Joanna's husband forget,
or seem to forget, that the story they
are telling their wives they have told them
before, word for word, their joy in the telling
their wives' joy as well—her own joy
as delicious as rereading a love letter,
as reassuring as sex, Joanna would like
to say to him. But if she were to suggest
he repeats himself, wouldn't her husband feel
the fool, wouldn't he tell her no story
that evening, or the next, until (at last)
in the kindness of time he forgot,
or seemed to forget, her indiscretion?
Isn't Joanna's pleasure equally
dependent upon his innocence, her
duplicity? Ah but now that the revolution
has, with all the charm of artillery,
burst upon their delicate garden,
shouldn't Joanna mistrust the old subterfuge,
isn't it *manipulation,* of the rouged
and high-heeled kind her daughters have,
in their intrepid march upon time, shed?
No, no, Joanna, the grandmothers whisper,
their ostrich fans aflutter, their puckered
elbows sheathed in dove grey leather, *this is
your function, this is how women survive.*

CIRCLES

Before her trip to the serpentarium,
back in the days when Joanna's concerns
were a wobbly diaphragm and coffee rings
on the rosewood table, she was still
sweetly reasonable; when the sun rose,
or the crocodile walked, she did not expect
a pirouette. In those moderate days
before Joanna took the leathersleeved
wheel of her Jaguar and drove herself to
the serpentarium, she never once
objected to Athena sprung from
the pink and ringleted head of Zeus,
or Eve dropped from Adam's fertile side.
In those restrained days before Joanna
purchased her ticket and stood up front, her
circles were still doodles, smileyfaces
whose lips were sealed, nests of circles in which
circles hid themselves, flourishes of missed
connections where, at the last moment, circles
lost their nerve. Back in those constrained
days before the curator opened the cage
and she saw opportunity look her in the eye,
Joanna would secretly pray for her life
to redo itself. But that was before
the day when, having been offered it,
Joanna grasped the cool writhing of a boa.

PANDORA JOANNA

Back to the ocean, the clamorer.
Back to sleeping with her ear to the mystery:
What gallops all day all night and gets not
a furlong farther? *Me,* Joanna says,
me when I seek myself. The ocean faces
her window is the wrong way to say it
but so what, Joanna is an American,
she can say anything she likes. She can
sit down at her dressing table and say
the sea is a blue flower lolling on
a reedy stem Joanna fingered a moment
and laid aside, satisfied her eyes were bluer.
She can say the moon is a white bee
in the blue flower withering (why not)
and the earth is an amber earring
on Joanna's dressing table. She can say
reason was Joanna's bumbling suitor
stung daft by the waning moon,
and Joanna reaching for her rouge is *wind*
whittling dry bee and flower. Without
a shred of evidence she can claim
she's the wind and the sea is her flower
and no doctor, no lawyer can put her away.
In the clear light of day even the Supreme Court
dare not rule the sun is *always* illumination,
never a gold bug that crawls on blue pages.

EEL WEATHER

At first it was fun, Joanna recalls.
Jokes about ark-building, feeling along
their necks for gills. But when morning after
morning rose only to its elbows, the days
phlegmier than Camille, then even
the cheeriest of Joanna's friends griped,
though the morbid among them seemed pleased.
Opinion is all, was Joanna's opinion.
Not so, the righteous objected, eel weather
comes from sin, and *kneeling* will turn the tide—
a silly stance, muttered the staunch, mopping
and wringing, hauling sandbags and sunlamps,
herding all dogpaddlers onto highground.
Far out and relaxed, the backfloaters
trusted *their* story—the sea has always
been involved with herself and only
incidentally with us. *Why run?* they sang
to Joanna as she yawed by, *doesn't
the willow look happy enough, and the gulls
plunging and plunging like the rain itself?*
Of course, sooner or later, everyone drowned,
even the backfloaters, even Joanna,
it was that sort of sea, wasn't it.
Well, what's done is done, Joanna said,
noting how green and extreme eel weather'd been,
something to write her grandchildren about.

STORIES SHE'S HEARD

In her youth, Joanna knew a journalist
who refused all sedation, determined to
cover even his death with perspicacity.
At the end, he curled like a scooped-out moon
and sang *Hush Little Baby,* but this was
all that he ever reported, and the part
about the moon is Joanna's invention.
Joanna's grandmother was 93
and putting death off, prompting death to seek
the aid of Joanna's great-grandfather
who lifted his daughter's wisp of white hair
and whispered into her stubborn ear,
Fanny, Fanny, you have nothing to fear,
weren't you always my favorite?
At 91, Thomas Everett Blasingame,
the oldest working cowboy in Texas,
lay down in a field and died the way he
said he should go, arms folded over his chest,
nearby a young horse he was training.
The posture for Zen monks to die in is sitting,
or, if enlightened, standing. Teng Yinfeng
stood on his head and his clothes rose
to cover his body, thus a great sacrilege to
carry him off for burning. The nun who was
his sister poked him with her finger
and he fell down with a bang.

TO THIS VERY DAY

Later, Joanna would insist her door
had been closed when the yogi walked through it.
And perhaps she is right, does it matter?
Does it matter that upon Joanna's Sarouk
he planted himself, and in spite of all
reasonable entreaties, he grew there,
in the center of the rug's medallion?
What thing can you name that can be explained?
(Why the archbishop? Why the tomato?)
At first the conservatory was ample,
the plant quiet enough, guests able to
move with a modicum of distraction
around the small brown body, sidestepping
shoots that mushroomed and ballooned, dismissing
fingery leaves that unwrapped themselves
to reveal nothing more startling
than themselves. At first, Joanna recalls,
the plant was ornamental, a jardiniere
(Gupta? Ming Dynasty?) being considered.
But as the proximity between plant
and Joanna grew, Joanna was forced from
the conservatory, out into the foyer
and past the sanctum of the library
where to this very day her husband's tongue
still moistens the tip of his pencil,
the next letter on its way to the puzzle.

THE YOGI'S DOG TELLS JOANNA

One winter my master walked me twice daily
past the lawn of the Unitarian Church
until (in bits and pieces) we learned
the people entering on Sunday mornings
were the American followers of Francis Davíd
the lucid martyr of west Transylvania,
but the people entering on Friday evenings
were the American followers of Delhi's
benevolent master Sant Darshan Singh,
while a few trees up we learned the people
entering the converted duplex next to
the Unitarian Church both mornings
and evenings were (so their contractor told us)
the American followers of Israel ben Eliezer
the exuberant Baal Shem of Mezhbezh,
distinctions which (my master says)
prepared us for those ripe summer months
when all the sacred doors and windows opened
and we heard the music of reason
and the music of ecstasy, and the music
of silence and the music of ecstasy
mingle more clearly than ever with
the music of cars and birds—a thing which
my master says (lifting his great sad eyes)
might be the last thing he utters
before he's allowed to stop uttering.

WHY DID JOANNA CROSS THE ROAD?

To get to the only side—an answer
not right, not wrong, but merely Joanna's
as she breathes deeply from her diaphragm
palms up on her bedroom floor, lotuslike.
Below, for good or for ill, a dog barks,
a car pulls into Joanna's courtyard.
The dog and the car become cutouts, flip
onto their sides, fly like cinematic
pages of time up from themselves and into
Joanna's mind where all the dogs and the cars
of her life have been expecting them,
a mind Joanna steps through, and ahead—
—No thing Joanna has known.
Neither meaning nor nonmeaning.
It opens her mouth, it bows her head.
It consumes her. The way night consumes
a moth, and space consumes the earth.
Joanna wants to prolong this endless
black dazzle, name it something wonderful—
the blind leap into the next second,
or *God.* She wants to press it like a rose,
paste it next to the dogs and the cars,
mail it to family and friends, as if it were
a thing separate from any one of them.
As if it could be shrunk to a thought Joanna
can walk down the stairs and answer the door in.

ROMANTIC JOANNA

Joanna has moved into the movie.
Beauty & Truth have taken her by the hand.
Nothing to fear, they whisper, the end will
return to the beginning, symmetry
will prevail, that's all she needs to know.
But when it comes, the end is shocking.
The end is way out of proportion.
The end is the end of everything.
The mad pursuit, the struggle to escape,
the gods, the trees, the happy, happy lovers—
all zapped, floating in the river of credits.
As the other patrons turn and chat and rise
and pass, Joanna sinks into her seat.
She cannot believe a whole world went blank.
Now she will have to go somewhere else,
do something else. Make up her *own* world.
She would like to discuss the details
over cappuccino and a kiwi tart—
what to put in, what to take out, things like that.
But Truth & Beauty are already in a taxi
to the next vision. Tarantino's perhaps,
or Kurosawa's. Whose doesn't matter.
Only that for ninety minutes or more, chaos
will be under control. A release
as great as death, these passionate lies
told in the dark one after the other.

JOANNA RAISES HER SHADE

So, heard the one about eternity?
Joanna wakes with a crick in her mind.
Seems she slept the wrong way, dreamt of death.
Eternity, she wails, her mind must find eternity
before it's too late. Where to begin.
Joanna shuffles her taffeta drapes,
she tugs her taffeta shade, pinkie adangle,
three fingers braced that graze her sill. Roused,
a fly buzzes. A mountain ash unfolds.
It crooks and splays, it splashes its fernery
in all directions at once while Joanna
is raising her shade. The mountain ash is
as fresh and sincere as a good idea,
like the notion of heaven, or socialism,
Joanna is thinking. Every morning
it shares a bit of sun, brings her news
of the wind, offers its good green ear.
But as Joanna's monkey mind reaches for the tree
—the shade snaps from her grip and spins—
as if the proper raising of her shade
were a matter of cosmic urgency,
a ceremony from which all things issue,
Joanna is thinking. Or perhaps this is not
quite what Joanna is thinking, thinking
being a language difficult to translate,
luminous arcs, most of them lost.